20 Clarinet Duets from Baroque to the 20th Century

MB99068

By Norman M. Heim

For Recital, Church or School Programs

© 2010 BY MEL BAY PUBLICATIONS, INC., PACIFIC, MO 63069.
ALL RIGHTS RESERVED. INTERNATIONAL COPYRIGHT SECURED. B.M.I. MADE AND PRINTED IN U.S.A.
No part of this publication may be reproduced in whole or in part, or stored in a retrieval system, or transmitted in any form
or by any means, electronic, mechanical, photocopy, recording, or otherwise, without written permission of the publisher.

Visit us on the Web at www.melbay.com or www.billsmusicshelf.com

Most duet books for clarinet consist of music from one historical period, or feature the music of one composer. This volume has works arranged for two clarinets, from each period starting with the Baroque and continuing into the twentieth century.

These duets are intended for the intermediate level clarinetist and can be played by junior and senior high school students. The music has been composed by well-known composers from about 1725-1900. These duets can be performed on recital or at church school or festival occasions.

Dr. Norman Heim
Gaithersburg, Maryland

Table of Contents

1. Pastoral Symphony(Messiah)---George F. Handel	4
2. Bourre from Fireworcs----George F. Handel	6
3. Sheep May Safely Graze---Johann S. Bach	7
4. Sarabande No. 1 and 2 --- Johann S. Bach	10
5. March from Musical Clocks --- Franz J. Haydn	12
6. Sonate No. 7 --- Franz J. Haydn	13
7. Romanze from Concerto K447 --- Wolfgang A. Mozart	16
8. Minuet K.331 --- Wolfgang A. Mozart	20
9. When Jesus Wept --- William Billings	26
10. Bagatelle op. 119, No. 1 --- Ludwig von Beethoven	28
11. Minuet in G --- Ludwig von Beethoven	32
12. Canon I --- Muzio Clemente	34
13. Canon II --- Muzio Clemente	36
14. Duet from Lakme --- Leo Delibes	40
15. Song Without Words (Folk Song) --- Felix Mendelssohn	42
16. Song Without Words op. 102, No. 6 --- Felix Mendelssohn	44
17. Lo, A Rose is Blooming -- Johannes Brahms	46
18. Song, op. 71, No. 2 --- Johannes Brahms	48
19. Dance (1999) -- Norman Heim	52
20. Pastorale (1999) -- Norman Heim	54

1. Pastoral Symphony (Messiah)

George F. Handel

2. Bouree from Fireworks

George F. Handel

3. Sheep May Safely Graze

Johann S. Bach
arranged by N. Heim

4. Sarabande No. 1

Johann S. Bach

Sarabande No. 2

Johann S. Bach

5. March from Musical Clocks

Franz J. Haydn

6. Sonate No. 7

Franz J. Haydn

7. Romanze from Concerto K447

Wolfgang A. Mozart

8. Minuet K.331

Wolfgang A. Mozart

This page has been left blank
to avoid awkward page turns.

9. When Jesus Wept

William Billings
arranged by N. Heim

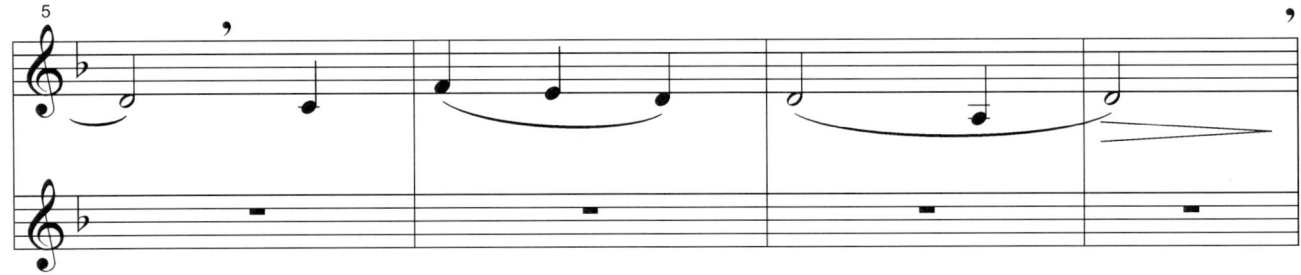

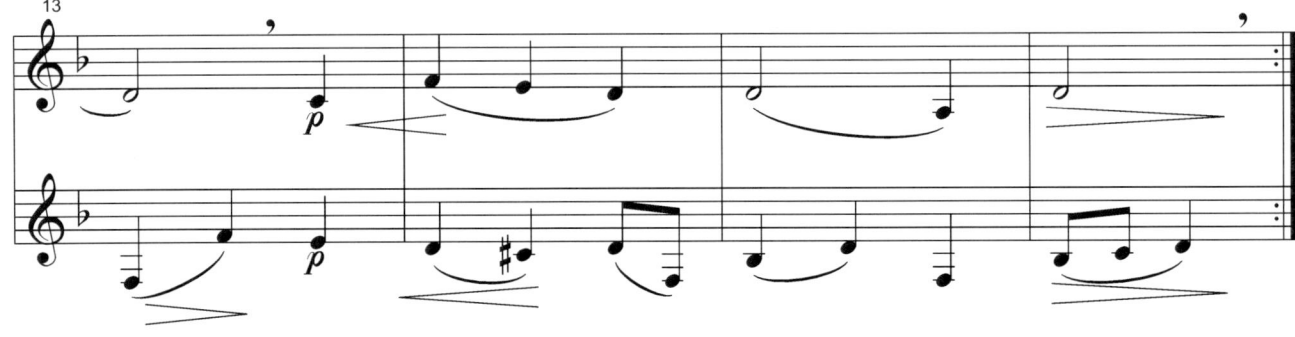
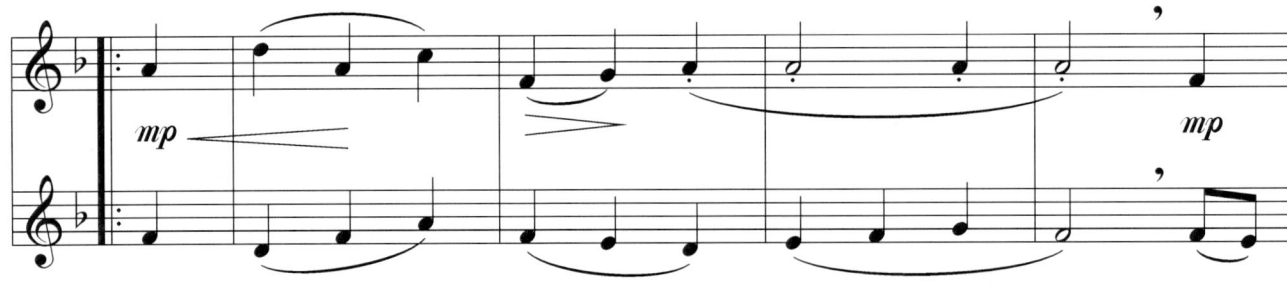

10. Bagatelle op. 119, No. 1

Ludwig von Beethoven

This page has been left blank
to avoid awkward page turns.

11. Minuet in G

Ludwig von Beethoven

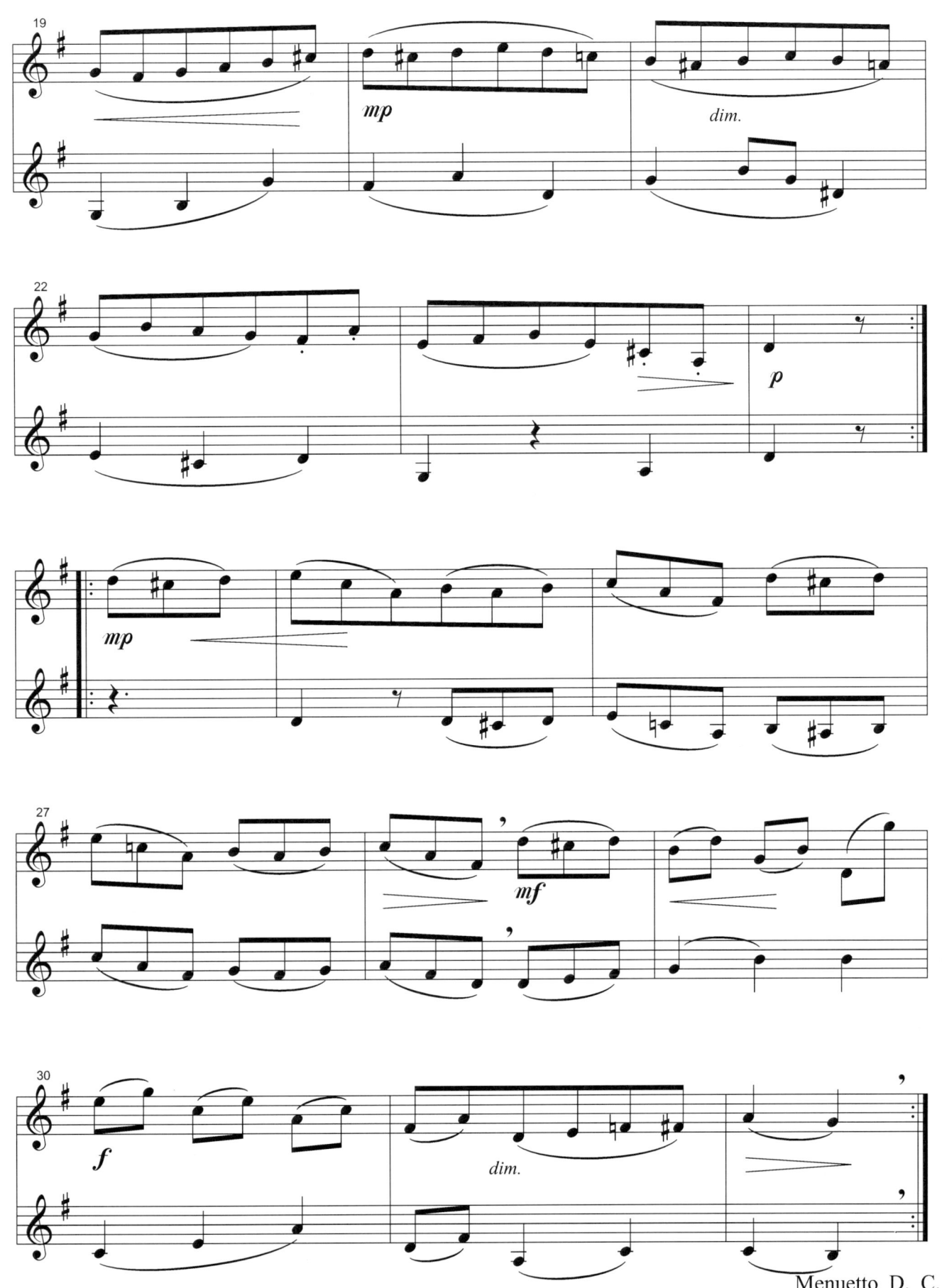

Menuetto D. C.

12.Canon I

Muzio Clemente

13. Canon II

Muzio Clemente

This page has been left blank
to avoid awkward page turns.

14. Duet from Lakme

Leo Delibes

15. Song Without Words (Folk Song)

Felix Mendelssohn

43

16. Song Without Words op. 102, No. 6

Felix Mendelssohn

17. Lo, A Rose is Blooming

Johannes Brahms

18. Song, op. 71, No. 2

Johannes Brahms

49

This page has been left blank to avoid awkward page turns.

19. Dance (1999)

Norman Heim

20. Pastorale (1999)

Norman Heim

UNIQUELY INTERESTING MUSIC !